DECODING CSS3

Learn to Design Beautiful Websites in 7 Days

AYUSH RAGHUWANSHI

*This book is dedicated to every Individual
who takes one more leap,
every time he encounters a failure.*

Preface

Before you dive into this book and embark on your journey into the world of web development, I urge you to first explore the foundational knowledge offered in the initial book of the *7 Days to Web Mastery* series: **DECODING HTML5: Learn to Create Beautiful Websites in 7 Days**. This first book will provide you with essential insights into HTML, which serves as the fundamental language of the web. Understanding HTML is akin to mastering the building blocks of web development, setting a solid foundation for your future endeavors in creating dynamic and visually appealing websites.

By taking the time to study and grasp the concepts presented in "DECODING HTML5," you'll be equipped with the necessary skills to proceed confidently to the next book in the series. This sequential approach ensures that you have a comprehensive understanding, enabling you to create functional and well-designed websites. So, invest the next seven days in absorbing the knowledge from "DECODING HTML5," and when you return, you'll be well-prepared to delve deeper into the world of web development with the subsequent book in the series.

Prepare yourself to unlock the potential of HTML5 and lay the groundwork for your journey to web mastery. Whether you're a beginner or looking to enhance your existing skills, this series offers a structured and insightful path to becoming proficient in web development. Start with "DECODING HTML5" and set yourself on the path to creating impressive websites with confidence and skill.

Disclaimer

This book is written and designed in such a way that the reader makes the most out of it while understanding new concepts within seven days. Do not get overwhelmed initially with the content which might seem alien and complex at first. You can take your time, move at your own pace, and finish the book. The objective is not to rush through the book but to acquire enough knowledge and apply it in different settings.

CONTENTS

Day 1

1. Introduction

After learning the basics of building a website i.e., **HTML**. There arises a need for designing the website because HTML itself does not contain any styling by default and it looks very ugly to display the contents, etc. on your website. To solve this problem of styling, **CSS** comes to our aid and styles our HTML web page to look beautiful and increase friendliness to the user.

Below are the two web pages with and without CSS:

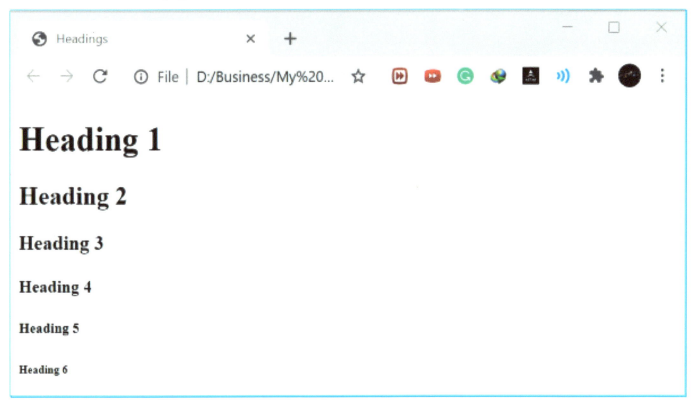

Fig 1.1 Web Page without CSS

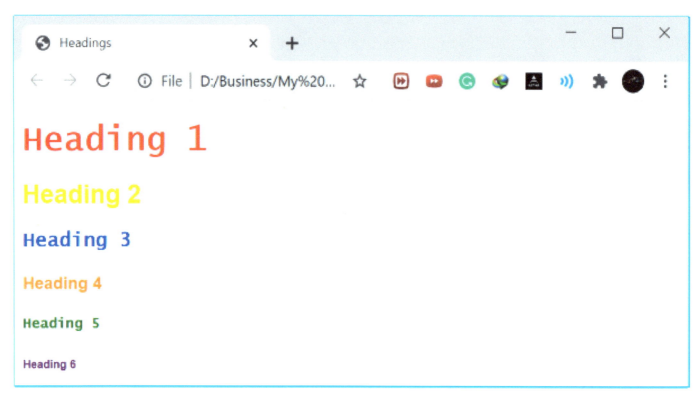

Fig 1.2 Web Page with CSS

2. Getting Started With CSS3

CSS is short for Cascading Style Sheets, used with **HTML** to increase the overall look and feel of the content on a web page. The latest version of CSS which is used currently almost everywhere is CSS 3 which provides Better styling, New transitions & animations, shadows, responsive layouts, embedded fonts, etc. than its previous versions.

There are three ways in which we can add CSS to our HTML documents:

1. **Inline CSS**
2. **Internal CSS**
3. **External CSS**

Commonly used by advanced developers is the External CSS because if you have a large website/project then External CSS is preferred to keep it separate from the HTML document. If the website/project is small to medium in length then Internal CSS is preferably used to avoid missing to add some designs to different contents. We will use Internal CSS throughout this book. CSS is declared under **<style>** tag which comes under **<head>** tag in HTML.

Syntax to declare CSS:

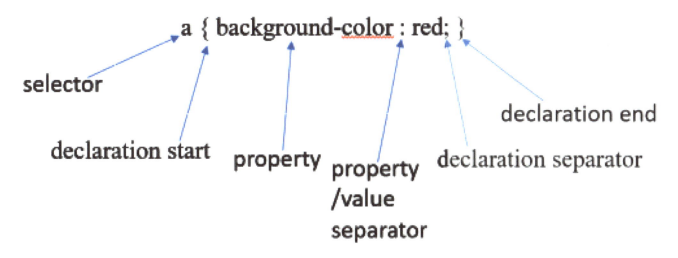

Fig 2.1 Syntax declaration in CSS

An Instance of Code 2.1 (for Fig 1.2) is shown below:

<!DOCTYPE html>

<html>

<head>

<title> Headings with CSS

</title>

```
<style>
h1 {
color: red;
font-family: "Lucida Console", "Courier New", monospace;
}
h2 {
color: yellow;
font-family: Arial, Helvetica, sans-serif;
}
h3 {
color: blue;
font-family: "Lucida Console", "Courier New", monospace;
}
h4 {
color: orange;
font-family: Arial, Helvetica, sans-serif;
}
h5 {
color: green;
font-family: "Lucida Console", "Courier New", monospace;
}
h6 {
color: purple;
font-family: Arial, Helvetica, sans-serif;
}
</style>
</head>
<body>
<!-- Headings -->
<h1>Heading 1</h1>
<h2>Heading 2</h2>
<h3>Heading 3</h3>
<h4>Heading 4</h4>
<h5>Heading 5</h5>
```

```
<h6>Heading 6</h6>
</body>
</html>
```

Comments in CSS are declared as:

/* This is a Comment. */

Units in CSS

There are two types of units in CSS that will be used throughout the book.

Absolute units:

- cm- Centimeters
- mm- Millimeters
- in- Inches

- px- Pixels (1px = 1/96th of 1in)
- pt- Points (1pt = 1/72 of 1in)
- pc- Picas picas (1pc = 12pt)

Relative units:

- %- with respect to the parent element
- em- with respect to font-size of the parent element
- rem- with respect to font size of the root element
- vw- with respect to 1% of viewport width
- vh- with respect to 1% of viewport height

Day 2

3. Basic Selectors

There are three types of selectors used in CSS: **Element** Selectors, **Multiple** Selectors, and **Nested** Selectors.

Element selectors are of three types:

1. . (for classes)
2. # (for IDs)
3. * (Universal selector)

An Instance of Code 3.1 is shown below:

```
<!DOCTYPE html>

<html>

<head> <title> CSS Selectors </title>

<style>
/* Element Selectors */
  body {
    background-color: #333;
  }
  /* . is for classes */
  .primary-heading {
    color: orange;
  }
  /* # is for IDs */
  #welcome {
    background-color: #f4f4f4;
  }
  /* Multiple Selectors */
  #welcome, #about {
    font-family: "Lucida Console", "Courier New", monospace;
  }
  /* Nested Selectors */
  #welcome p {
    font-family: Arial, Helvetica, sans-serif;
```

```
    }
    #about {
      color: white;
    }
</style> </head>
<body>
<div id="welcome">
    <h2 class="primary-heading">Welcome</h2>
    <p>Lorem ipsum dolor sit amet consectetur adipisicing elit. Quod qui iusto perferendis nisi officia quidem ad enim maiores animi maxime.</p>
  </div>
  <div id="about">
    <h2>About</h2>
    <p>Lorem ipsum dolor sit amet consectetur adipisicing elit. Eveniet laudantium voluptatum dolorum iure, eos et distinctio porro provident ut assumenda.</p>
  </div>
</body>
</html>
```

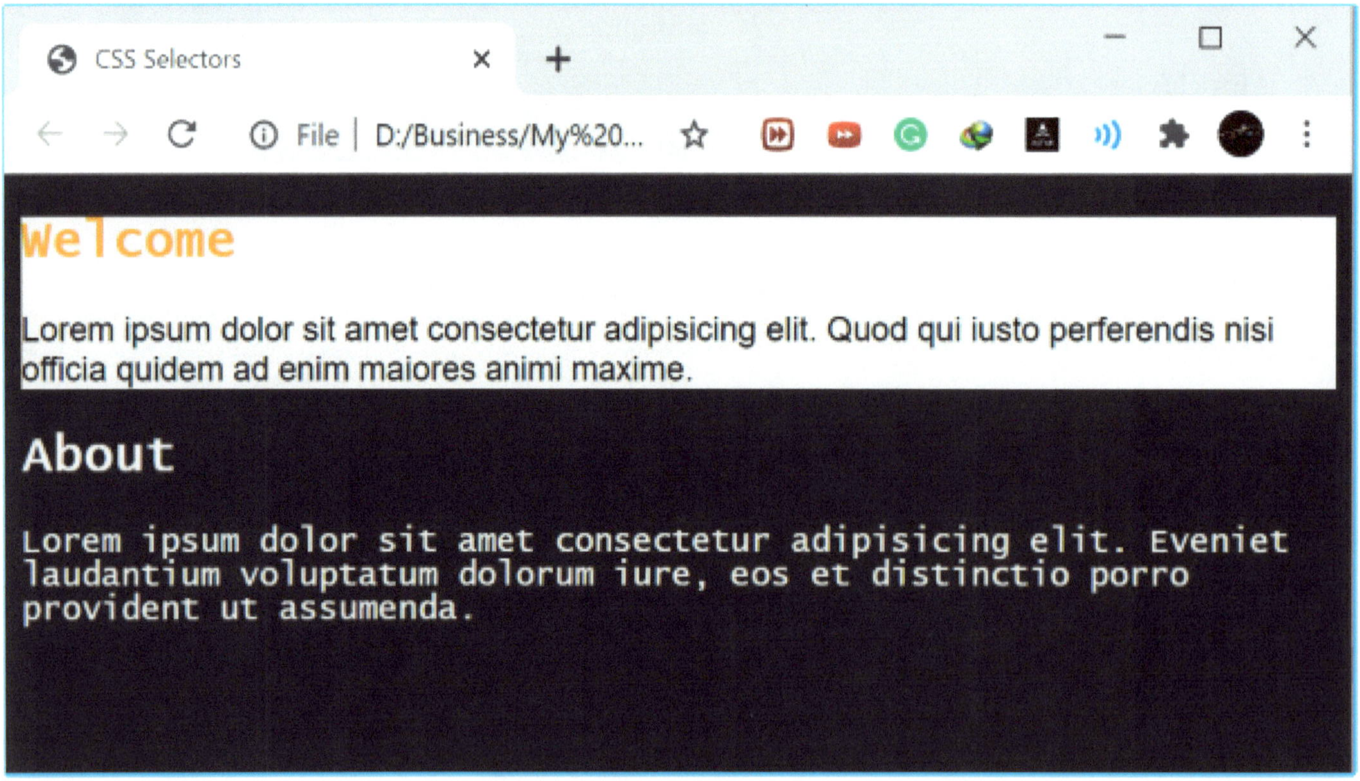

Fig 3.1 Output for Code 3.1

4. Fonts

Fonts are used to display the text beautifully to the user and according to our need and it also increases the readability. Fonts (with their values) in CSS are of the following types:

- **Size** (large, larger, medium, small, smaller, x-large, x-small)
- **Family** ({Arial, Helvetica, sans-serif}, {"Arial Black", Gadget, sans-serif}, {"Bookman Old Style", serif}, {"Comic Sans MS" cursive, sans-serif}, {Courier, monospace}, {"Courier New", Courier, monospace}, {Garamond, serif}, {Georgia, serif}, {Impact, Charcoal, sans-serif}, {"Lucida Console", Monaco, monospace}, {"Lucida Sans Unicode", "Lucida Grande", sans-serif}, {"MS Sans Serif", Geneva, sans-serif}, {"MS Sans Serif", "New York", sans-serif}, {"Palatino Linotype", "Book Antiqua", Palatino, serif}, {Tahoma, Geneva, sans-serif}, {"Times New Roman", Times, serif}, {"Trebuchet MS", Helvetica, sans-serif}, {Verdana, Geneva, sans-serif}) – These fonts are supported by almost all web browsers.
- **Weight** (100, 200, 300, 900, bold, bolder, lighter)
- **Style** (italic, normal, oblique, inherit, initial, unset)
- **Variant** (normal, small-caps, inherit, initial, unset)

An Instance of Code 4.1 is shown below:

```
<!DOCTYPE html>
<html>
<head>
  <title>Fonts
</title>
  <style>
    body {
      font-family: Arial, Helvetica, sans-serif;
      font-size: x-large;
    }

    #welcome p span {
      font-weight: bold;
      font-variant: small-caps;
```

```
    }

    #about p span {
      font-style: italic;
    }
  </style>
</head>

<body>
  <div id="welcome">
    <h2 class="primary-heading">Welcome</h2>
    <p>Lorem ipsum dolor sit amet consectetur adipisicing elit. <span>Quod qui iusto perferendis nisi officia quidem ad enim</span> maiores animi maxime.</p>
  </div>

  <div id="about">
    <h2>About</h2>
    <p>Lorem ipsum dolor sit amet consectetur adipisicing elit.<span>Eveniet laudantium voluptatum dolorum iure,</span> eos et distinctio porro provident ut assumenda.</p>
  </div>
</body>
</html>
```

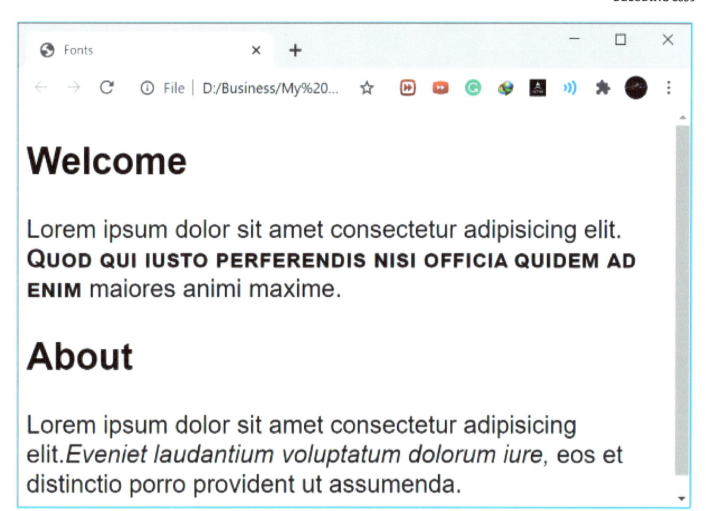

Fig 4.1 Output for Code 4.1

Day 3

5. Color Types

Three types of color types are used in CSS to define which color we want our text or button to look like.

1. Directly specifying the **color name**.
2. Giving the **RGB values** which range from **0-255**.
3. Declaring **Hexadecimal (or hex) values** of colors.

The syntax for all the color types used in CSS (in order):

1. color: red;
2. color: rgb(255,0,255);
3. color: #f4f4f4;

RGB values for some colors used commonly are:

Color Name	Color Code (RGB)
Red	(255,0,0)
Blue	(0,0,255)
Yellow	(255,255,0)
Green	(0,128,0)
Grey	(128,128,128)
Black	(0,0,0)
Pink	(255,192,203)
Cyan	(0,255,255)
Magenta	(255,0,255)

Hexadecimal values for some colors used commonly are:

Color Name	Color Code (hexadecimal)
Red	#FF0000
Blue	#0000FF
Yellow	#FFFF00
Green	#008000
Grey	#808080
Black	#000000
Pink	#FFC0CB
Cyan	#00FFFF

Magenta	#FF00FF

For more Color codes follow this website: https://www.color-hex.com/

An Instance of Code 5.1 is shown below:

```
<!DOCTYPE html>
<html>
<head> <title>Color Types</title>
  <style>
    h1 {
      /* Color Name */
      color: red;
    }
    h2 {
      /* RGB */
      color: rgb(0,128,255);
    }
    h3 {
      /* Hex */
      color: #00FFFF;
    }
  </style> </head>
<body>
  <h1>Heading One</h1>
  <h2>Heading Two</h2>
  <h3>Heading Three</h3>
</body>
</html>
```

Fig 5.1 Output for Code 5.1

6. Backgrounds & Borders

The **background** in CSS can have a background color or a background image. The background color is just a solid color that can be added to any text, background, etc, in CSS. PNG files can have a transparent background but JPG/JPEG files only have solid colors/backgrounds.

Syntax to give a background color:

background-color: red;

Syntax to give a background image:

background: url('./img/leaf.png');

More properties can be given in the background image such as repeat or no-repeat, position, and size.

Syntax to give a background image (additional properties):

1. **background-image: url('./img/leaf.png');**

   background-repeat: no-repeat;

   background-position: center top;

   background-size: cover;

2. **background: url('./img/leaf.png') no-repeat center center/cover;**

Any one of the syntaxes can be used to display a background image.

The **Border** is specified to contain the text, image, etc. We need to specify three attributes while using the border: Width, Color, and Style.

Syntax to give border:

1. **border-width: 3px;**

   border-color: red;

   border-style: solid;

2. **border: 3px solid red;**

Any one of the syntaxes can be used to display a border.

An Instance of Code 6.1 is shown below:

```
<!DOCTYPE html>
<html>
```

```
<head>
  <title>Backgrounds & Borders</title>
  <style>
    #box-1 {
      background-color: blanchedalmond;
      border: 3px solid red;
      border-radius: 10px;
    }
    #box-2 {
      background: #333;
      color: #fff;
      border-top: blue solid 3px;
      border-top-left-radius: 10px;
      border-top-right-radius: 10px;
    }
    #box-3 {
      /* background-image: url('./img/stars.jpg');
      background-repeat: no-repeat;
      background-position: center top;
      background-size: cover; */
      background: url('./img/stars.jpg') no-repeat center center/cover;
      color: #fff;
      height: 300px;
      width: 600px;
    }
    #box-4 {
      background: url('./img/leaf.png') no-repeat center center;
      background-attachment: fixed;
    }
  </style>
</head>
<body>
  <div id="box-1">
    <h3>Box One</h3>
```

```
    <p>Lorem ipsum dolor sit, amet consectetur adipisicing elit. Repudiandae quia possimus harum labore voluptatem. Praesentium rerum sint eaque blanditiis et.</p>
  </div>
  <br>
  <div id="box-2">
    <h3>Box Two</h3>
    <p>Lorem ipsum dolor sit, amet consectetur adipisicing elit. Repudiandae quia possimus harum labore voluptatem. Praesentium rerum sint eaque blanditiis et.</p>
  </div>
  <div id="box-3">
    <h3>Box Three</h3>
    <p>Lorem ipsum dolor sit, amet consectetur adipisicing elit. Repudiandae quia possimus harum labore voluptatem. Praesentium rerum sint eaque blanditiis et.</p>
  </div>
  <div id="box-4">
    <h3>Box Four</h3>
    <p>Lorem ipsum dolor sit, amet consectetur adipisicing elit. Repudiandae quia possimus harum labore voluptatem. Praesentium rerum sint eaque blanditiis et.</p>
    <p>Lorem ipsum dolor sit, amet consectetur adipisicing elit. Repudiandae quia possimus harum labore voluptatem. Praesentium rerum sint eaque blanditiis et.</p>
    <p>Lorem ipsum dolor sit, amet consectetur adipisicing elit. Repudiandae quia possimus harum labore voluptatem. Praesentium rerum sint eaque blanditiis et.</p>
    <p>Lorem ipsum dolor sit, amet consectetur adipisicing elit. Repudiandae quia possimus harum labore voluptatem. Praesentium rerum sint eaque blanditiis et.</p>
    <p>Lorem ipsum dolor sit, amet consectetur adipisicing elit. Repudiandae quia possimus harum labore voluptatem. Praesentium rerum sint eaque blanditiis et.</p>
    <p>Lorem ipsum dolor sit, amet consectetur adipisicing elit. Repudiandae quia possimus harum labore voluptatem. Praesentium rerum sint eaque blanditiis et.</p>
    <p>Lorem ipsum dolor sit, amet consectetur adipisicing elit. Repudiandae quia possimus harum labore voluptatem. Praesentium rerum sint eaque blanditiis et.</p>
  </div>
</body>
</html>
```

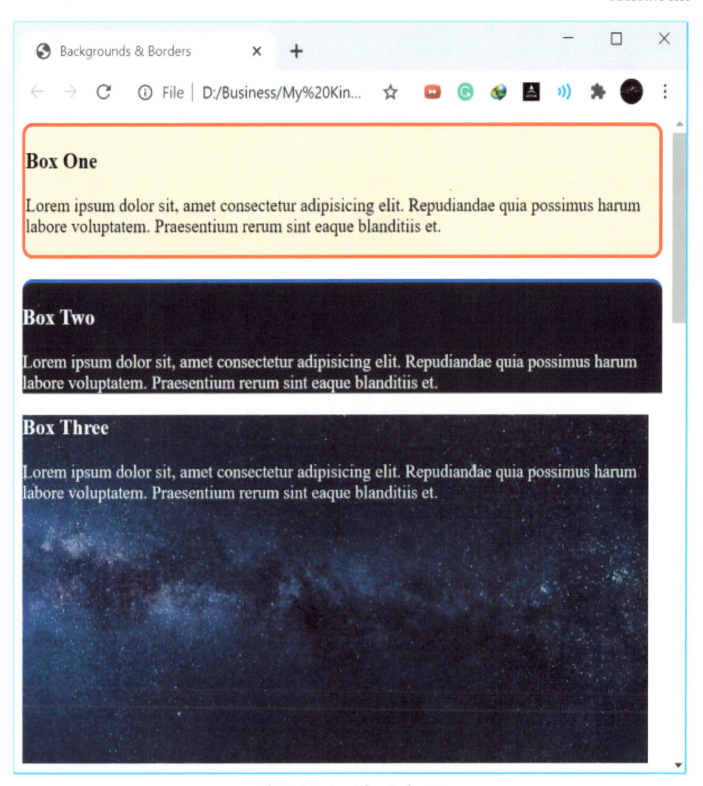

Fig 6.1 Output for Code 6.1

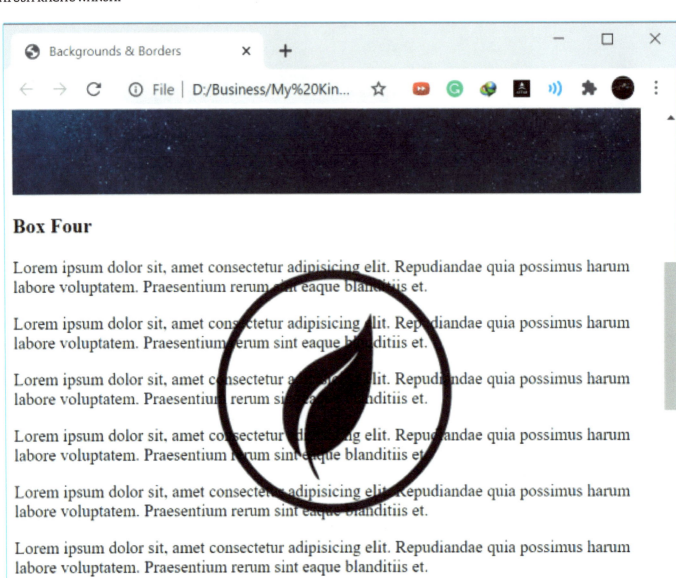

Fig 6.2 Output for Code 6.1 (continue)

Day 4

7. Box Model, Margin & Padding

Box/Box model is defined in IDs or classes in CSS to contain any text or image inside it and properties are added to this box so that every item inside it gets affected in one go.

Syntax to define a box:

.box {

background: #F4F4F4;

border: 2px #777 solid;

width: 500px;

}

Margin is defined as the space around, or outside defined borders of a text, image, box, etc. There are four properties to define a margin:

1. **margin-top**
2. **margin-right**
3. **margin-bottom**
4. **margin-left**

Syntax to define a margin:

margin-top: 10px;

margin-right: 20px;

margin-bottom: 40px;

margin-left: 20px;

Padding is defined as the space created around any text, image, etc. inside any defined borders. There are four properties to define a padding:

1. **padding-top**
2. **padding-right**
3. **padding-bottom**
4. **padding-left**

Syntax to define a padding:

padding-top: 10px;

padding-right: 20px;

padding-bottom: 40px;

padding-left: 20px;

An Instance of Code 7.1 is shown below:

```html
<!DOCTYPE html>
<html>
<head>
  <title>Box Model, Margin & Padding</title>
  <style>
    /* CSS Reset */
    * {
      margin: 0;
      padding: 0;
      box-sizing: border-box;
    }
    .box {
      background: #f4f4f4;
      border: 2px #777 solid;
      width: 500px;
      /* Padding on all sides */
      padding: 20px;
      /* Padding per side */
      padding-top: 10px;
      padding-right: 20px;
      padding-bottom: 10px;
      padding-left: 20px;
      /* Padding shorthand = top, right, bottom, left */
      padding: 10px 20px 10px 20px;
      /* Padding shorthand = top/bottom left/right */
      padding: 10px 20px;
      /* Margin on all sides */
      margin: 20px;
      /* Margin per side */
      margin-top: 10px;
      margin-right: 20px;
      margin-bottom: 10px;
```

```
      margin-left: 20px;
      /* Margin shorthand = top, right, bottom, left */
      margin: 10px 20px 10px 20px;
      /* Margin shorthand = top/bottom left/right */
      margin: 10px 20px;
    }
    .box h3 {
      padding-bottom: 10px;
    }
  </style>
</head>
<body>
  <div class="box">
    <h3>Box One</h3>
    <p>Lorem ipsum dolor sit amet consectetur adipisicing elit. Ipsum nulla beatae id, dolorum accusamus neque atque similique consectetur eaque odio?</p>
  </div>
  <div class="box">
    <h3>Box Two</h3>
    <p>Lorem ipsum dolor sit amet consectetur adipisicing elit. Ipsum nulla beatae id, dolorum accusamus neque atque similique consectetur eaque odio?</p>
  </div>
</body>
</html>
```

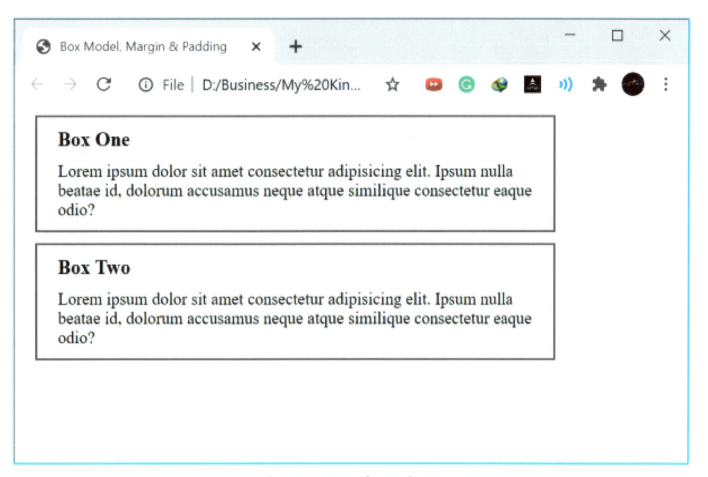

Fig 7.1 Output for Code 7.1

8. Float & Alignment

The **Float** property in CSS specifies how the element should float on the web page. We can specify the direction with some additional parameters like:

1. inline-end
2. inline-start
3. left
4. none
5. right
6. inherit
7. initial
8. unset

Syntax to define float:

.box1 {

float: left;

width: 60%;

}

.box2 {

float: right;

width: 40%;

}

The **Clear** property is also used with the float to specify what element can float next to the cleared element and on which side.

The **Alignment** property is used in CSS to align the text horizontally with some parameters like:

1. center
2. end
3. justify
4. left
5. right
6. start
7. inherit
8. initial
9. unset

Syntax to define alignment:

#box p {

```
text-align: left;
width: 50%;
}
```

An Instance of Code 8.1 is shown below:

```html
<!DOCTYPE html>
<html>
<head>
  <title>Float & Alignment</title>
  <style>
    * {
      box-sizing: border-box;
    }
    body {
      font-family: Arial, Helvetica, sans-serif;
      line-height: 1.4em;
    }
    .container {
      max-width: 960px;
      margin: 30px auto;
    }
    .clr {
      clear: both;
    }
    .box {
      background: #f4f4f4;
      border: 1px solid #333;
      padding: 20px;
      margin-bottom: 15px;
    }
    .box p {
      /* Text Align */
      text-align: left;
      text-align: right;
```

```
      text-align: center;
      text-align: justify;
    }
    #box-2 {
      float: left;
      width: 68%;
    }
    #box-3 {
      float: right;
      width: 30%;
    }
  </style>
</head>
<body>
  <div class="container">
    <div id="box-1" class="box">
      <h3>Heading</h3>
      <p>Lorem ipsum dolor sit amet consectetur adipisicing elit. Rem dolor, soluta esse voluptas aliquam eligendi veritatis illo impedit minus unde.</p>
    </div>
    <div id="box-2" class="box">
      <h3>Heading</h3>
      <p>Lorem ipsum dolor sit amet consectetur adipisicing elit. Rem dolor, soluta esse voluptas aliquam eligendi veritatis illo impedit minus unde.</p>
    </div>
    <div id="box-3" class="box">
      <h3>Heading</h3>
      <p>Lorem ipsum dolor sit amet consectetur adipisicing elit. Rem dolor, soluta esse voluptas aliquam eligendi veritatis illo impedit minus unde.</p>
    </div>
    <div class="clr"></div>
    <div id="box-4" class="box">
      <h3>Heading</h3>
      <p>Lorem ipsum dolor sit amet consectetur adipisicing elit. Rem dolor, soluta esse voluptas aliquam eligendi veritatis illo impedit minus unde.</p>
```

```
  </div>
 </div>
</body>
</html>
```

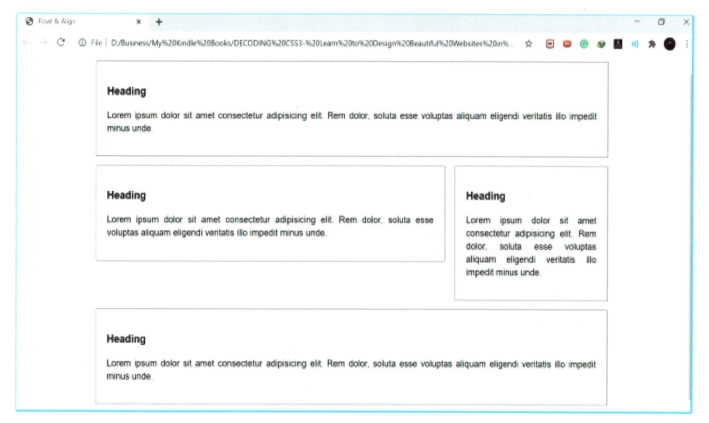

Fig 8.1 Output for Code 8.1

Day 5

9. Link State & Button Styling

Links are popularly used to navigate through web pages. In CSS we can style a link with multiple properties. A link has four states:

1. **Regular state**- By default state of the link.
2. **Hover state**- On placing the move over the link.
3. **Active state**- After the link is clicked.
4. **Visited state**- After the link is clicked and visited.

By default, a link appears blue with an underline. However, we can style it to look attractive by:

text-decoration: none;

And adding additional properties in CSS.

Buttons are also widely used on web pages. CSS provides many properties to style a button.

An Instance of Code 9.1 is shown below:

```
<!DOCTYPE html>
<html>
<head>
  <title>Links & Buttons</title>
  <style>
    body {
      font-family: "Trebuchet MS", Helvetica, sans-serif;
    }
    a {
      color: #333;
      text-decoration: none;
    }
    a:hover {
      color: coral;
    }
    /* a:visited {
      color: red;
    } */
```

```css
    a:active {
      color: red;
    }
    /* Button Styling */
    .btn {
      background: #4c6ca0;
      color: #fff;
      border: none;
      font-size: 16px;
      padding: 10px 20px;
      border-radius: 5px;
      cursor: pointer;
    }
    .btn:hover {
      color: #f4f4f4;
      background: #446190;
    }
  </style>
</head>
<body>
  <br>
  <a class="btn" href="#">Click Here</a>
  <br>
  <br>
  <button class="btn">New Button</button>
</body>
</html>
```

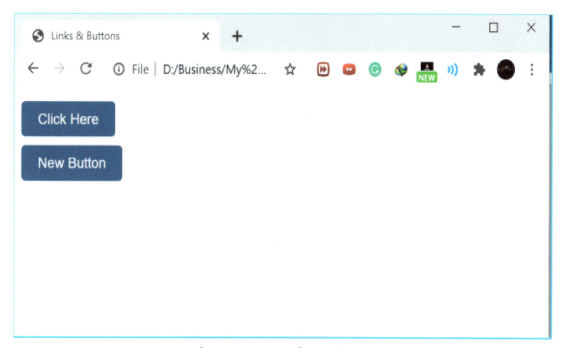

Fig 9.1 Output for Code 9.1

10. Navigation Menu Styling

A **Navigation Menu** is used in web pages to navigate through the page easily and quickly. CSS provides multiple properties to style a Navigation menu/bar using the **list-style** property:

1. armenian
2. circle
3. decimal
4. decimal-leading-zero
5. disc
6. georgian
7. inside
8. lower-alpha
9. lower-greek
10. lower-latin
11. lower-roman
12. none
13. outside
14. square
15. symbols()
16. upper-alpha
17. upper-latin
18. upper-roman
19. url()

An Instance of Code 10.1 is shown below:

```
<!DOCTYPE html>
<html>
<head>
  <title>Menu Styling</title>
  <style>
    body {
      font-family: "Courier New", Courier, monospace;
    }
    .navbar {
      list-style: none;
      margin: 0;
```

```css
  padding: 0;
  background: #4c6ca0;
  border-radius: 5px;
  overflow: auto;
}
.navbar li {
  float: left;
}
.navbar li a {
  display: block;
  color: #fff;
  text-decoration: none;
  padding: 15px 20px;
}
.navbar li a:hover {
  background-color: #446190;
  color: #f4f4f4;
}
.side-menu {
  list-style: none;
  border: 1px #ddd solid;
  border-radius: 10px;
  width: 300px;
  padding: 20px;
}
.side-menu li {
  font-size: 18px;
  line-height: 2.4em;
  border-bottom: dotted 1px #ddd;
}
.side-menu li:last-child {
  border: none;
}
.side-menu li a {
```

```
    color: #333;
    text-decoration: none;
  }
  .side-menu li a:hover {
    color: coral;
  }
 </style>
</head>
<body>
 <ul class="navbar">
  <li><a href="#">Home Page</a></li>
  <li><a href="#">Details</a></li>
  <li><a href="#">Services</a></li>
  <li><a href="#">Contacts</a></li>
 </ul>
 <br><br>
 <ul class="side-menu">
  <li><a href="#">Home Page</a></li>
  <li><a href="#">Details</a></li>
  <li><a href="#">Services</a></li>
  <li><a href="#">Contacts</a></li>
 </ul>
</body>
</html>
```

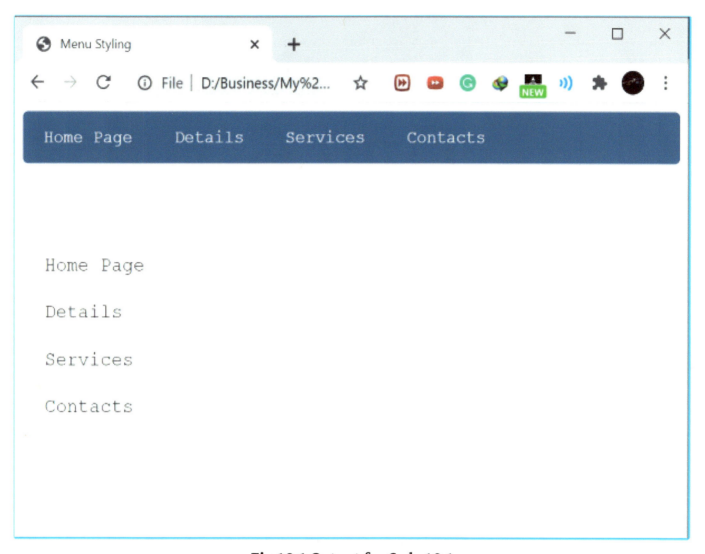

Fig 10.1 Output for Code 10.1

Day 6

11. Inline, Block & Inline-Block Display

There are three types of display properties in CSS:

1. **Inline level element**- Displays an element as an inline element, height and width properties will take no effect.
2. **Block level element**- Displays an element as a block, starts with a new line, and takes up the complete width.
3. **Inline-block level element**- Displays an element as an inline-block container, height and width will take effect.

Elements/tags that have an **Inline** property by default:

- span
- a
- img
- em
- strong
- i
- small

Fig. 11.1 \<a\> tag is an Inline element

Elements/tags that have a **block** property by default:

- div
- h1
- p
- li
- section

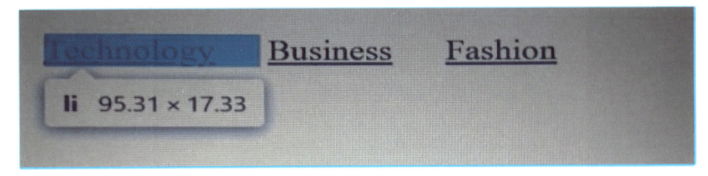

Fig. 11.2 <li> tag is a block element

Syntax to display properties:

#box1 {

display: inline-block;

width: 60%;

}

An Instance of Code 11.1 is shown below:

```
<!DOCTYPE html>
<html>
<head>
  <title>Inline, Block & Inline-Block Styling</title>
  <style>
    li {
      display: inline;
    }
    li a {
      padding-right: 20px;
    }
    img {
      display: block;
      margin: auto;
    }
    .box {
      width: 32.8%;
      display: inline-block;
      box-sizing: border-box;
      background: #f4f4f4;
```

```
      padding: 10px;
      margin-bottom: 10px;
    }
  </style>
</head>
<body>
  <ul>
    <li><a href="#">Technology</a></li>
    <li><a href="#">Business</a></li>
    <li><a href="#">Fashion</a></li> </ul><br>
  <img src="./img/leaf.png" alt="My image"><br>
  <div class="box">
    <h3>Heading</h3>
    <p>Lorem ipsum dolor sit amet consectetur adipisicing elit. Aspernatur iure in fugiat!</p>
  </div>
  <div class="box">
    <h3>Heading</h3>
    <p>Lorem ipsum dolor sit amet consectetur adipisicing elit. Aspernatur iure in fugiat!</p>
  </div>
  <div class="box">
    <h3>Heading</h3>
    <p>Lorem ipsum dolor sit amet consectetur adipisicing elit. Aspernatur iure in fugiat!/p>
  </div>
</body>
</html>
```

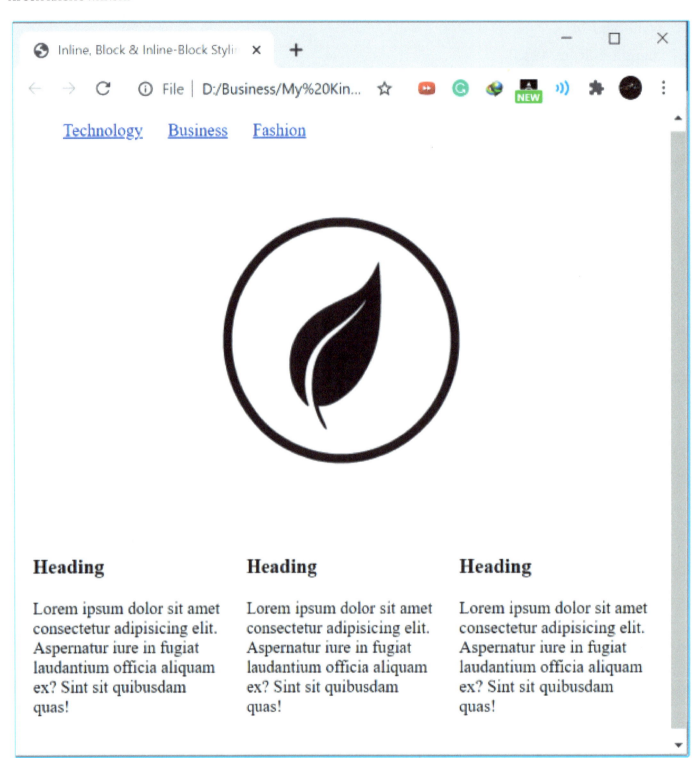

Fig 11.3 Output for Code 11.1

12. Positioning

The **Position** property in CSS specifies the type of positioning method used for an element. Different types of position values:

- static
- relative
- fixed
- absolute
- sticky

An Instance of Code 12.1 is shown below:

```
<!DOCTYPE html>
<html>
<head> <title>Positioning in CSS</title>
  <style>
    body {
      height: 4000px;
    }
    .box {
      width: 100px;
      height: 100px;
    }
    .container {
      position: relative;
      width: 500px;
      height: 400px;
      background: #333;
    }
    #box-1 {
      position: relative;
      top: 50px;
      left: 50px;
      z-index: 1;
```

```css
      background: red;
    }
    #box-2 {
      position: absolute;
      top: 100px;
      left: 100px;
      background: yellow;
    }
    #box-3 {
      position: absolute;
      bottom: 100px;
      right: 100px;
      background: green;
    }
    #box-4 {
      position: fixed;
      background: grey;
    }
    #box-5 {
      position: sticky;
      top: 0;
      background: orange;
      z-index: -1;
    } </style>
</head>
<body>
  <div id="box-1" class="box"></div>
  <div class="container">
    <div id="box-2" class="box"></div>
    <div id="box-3" class="box"></div> </div>
  <div id="box-4" class="box"></div>
  <div id="box-5" class="box"></div>
</body>
</html>
```

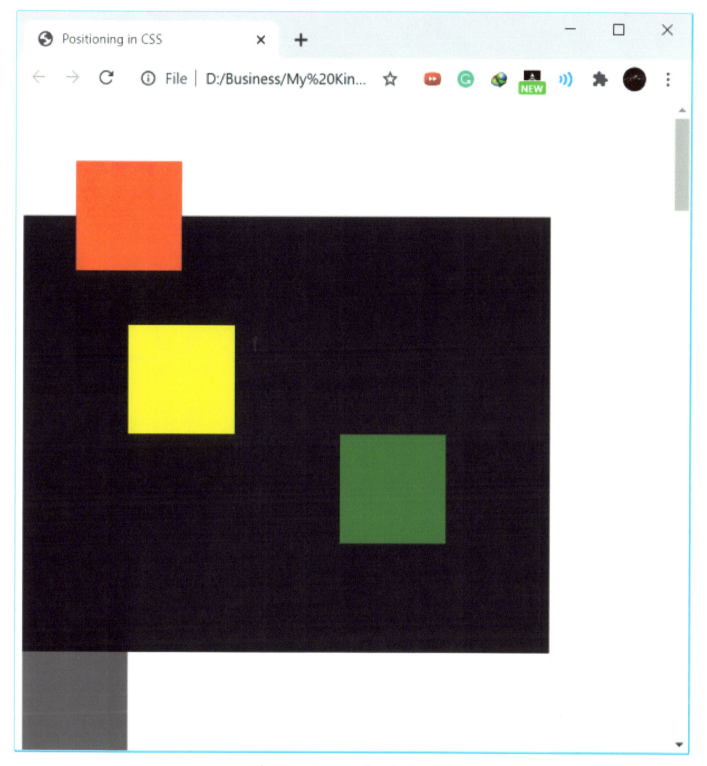

Fig 12.1 Output for Code 12.1

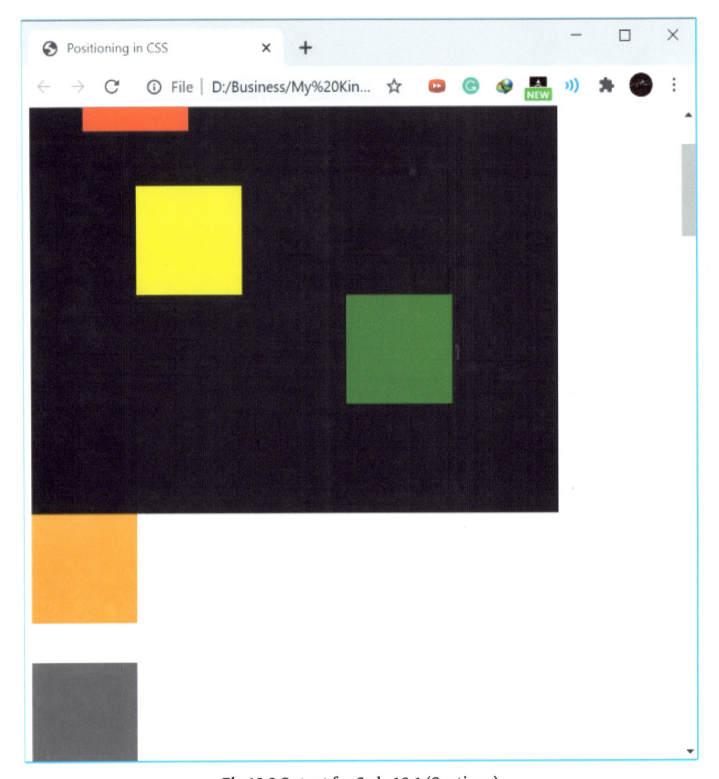

Fig 12.2 Output for Code 12.1 (Continue)

Day 7

13. Small Project- Styling A Form

Forms are used everywhere on the websites to collect information from the users. With CSS we can style a form beautifully to get attention from the people and get our work done.

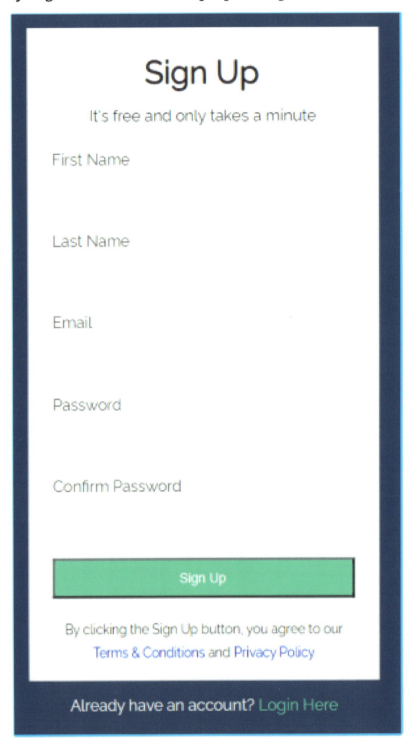

Fig 13.1 Sample Form

An Instance of Code 13.1 for Fig 13.1 is shown below:

```
<!DOCTYPE html>
<html>
  <head>
    <title>Form Styling</title>
    <link
      href="https://fonts.googleapis.com/css?family=Raleway"
      rel="stylesheet"
    />
    <style>
      * {
        box-sizing: border-box;
        margin:0;
        padding: 0;
      }
      body {
        font-family: 'Raleway', sans-serif;
        background: #344a72;
        color: #fff;
        line-height: 1.8;
      }
      a {
        text-decoration: none;
      }
      #container {
        margin: 30px auto;
        max-width: 400px;
        padding: 20px;
      }
      .form-wrap {
        background: #fff;
        padding: 15px 25px;
```

```css
    color: #333;
  }
  .form-wrap h1,
  .form-wrap p {
    text-align: center;
  }
  .form-wrap .form-group {
    margin-top: 15px;
  }
  .form-wrap .form-group label {
    display: block;
    color: #666;
  }
  .form-wrap .form-group input {
    width: 100%;
    padding: 10px;
    border: #ddd 1px solid;
    border-radius: 5px;
  }
  .form-wrap button {
    display: block;
    width: 100%;
    padding: 10px;
    margin-top: 20px;
    background: #49c1a2;
    color: #fff;
    cursor: pointer;
  }
  .form-wrap button:hover {
    background: #37a08e
  }
  .form-wrap .bottom-text {
    font-size: 13px;
    margin-top: 20px;
```

```
      }
      footer {
        text-align: center;
        margin-top: 10px;
      }
      footer a {
        color:#49c1a2
      }
    </style>
  </head>
  <body>
    <div id="container">
      <div class="form-wrap">
        <h1>Sign Up</h1>
        <p>It's free and only takes a minute</p>
        <form>
          <div class="form-group">
              <label for="first-name">First Name</label>
              <input type="text" name="firstName" id="first-name" />
          </div>
          <div class="form-group">
              <label for="last-name">Last Name</label>
              <input type="text" name="lastName" id="last-name" />
          </div>
          <div class="form-group">
              <label for="email">Email</label>
              <input type="email" name="email" id="email" />
          </div>
          <div class="form-group">
              <label for="password">Password</label>
              <input type="password" name="password" id="password" />
          </div>
          <div class="form-group">
              <label for="password2">Confirm Password</label>
```

```
            <input type="password" name="pasword2" id="password2" />
        </div>
        <button type="submit" class="btn">Sign Up</button>
        <p class="bottom-text">
                By clicking the Sign Up button, you agree to our
                <a href="#">Terms & Conditions</a> and
                <a href="#">Privacy Policy</a>
        </p>
    </form>
  </div>
  <footer>
    <p>Already have an account? <a href="#">Login Here</a></p>
  </footer>
 </div>
 </body>
</html>
```

14. Visibility, Order & Negative Margin

There are chances while using CSS that you first give color (red) to a heading element and afterward you give a different color (blue) to the class of the heading element. The second color (blue) given might override the previously given color (red). To overcome such situations, we can use-**! important** flag after giving the color (red) in the first heading element to reduce overriding.

An Instance of Code 14.1 is shown below:

```
<!DOCTYPE html>
<html>
<head>
  <title>Visibility and Order</title>
  <style>
    h1 {
        color: blue !important;
        }
    .hello {
        color: red;
        }
  </style>
</head>
<body>
    <h1>Hello World!</h1>
    <p>Lorem ipsum dolor sit amet consectetur adipisicing elit. Ipsum nulla beatae id, dolorum accusamus neque atque similique consectetur eaque odio?</p>
</body>
</html>
```

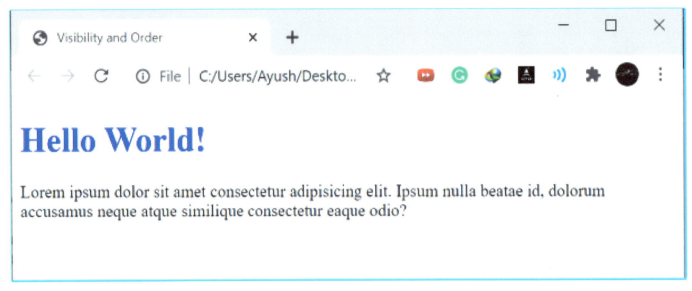

Fig 14.1 Output for Code 14.1

The **Negative Margin** concept is used in CSS just to display some part of the text or just to highlight the text as the web page loads.

An Instance of Code 14.2 is shown below:

```
<!DOCTYPE html>
<html>
<head>
  <title>Negative Margin</title>
  <style>
  h1 {
      color: blue !important;
      }
  .hello {
      color: red;
      margin-top: -20px;
      margin-left: -20px;
      }
  .welcome {
      color: yellow;
      margin-top: 30px;
      margin-left: 30px;
      }
```

```
    </style>
</head>
<body>
    <h1 class="hello">Hello World!</h1>
    <p>Lorem ipsum dolor sit amet consectetur adipisicing elit.
Ipsum nulla beatae id, dolorum accusamus neque atque similique
consectetur eaque odio?</p>
    <h1 class="welcome">Welcome!</h1>
    <p>Lorem ipsum dolor sit amet consectetur adipisicing elit.
Ipsum nulla beatae id, dolorum accusamus neque atque similique
consectetur eaque odio?</p>
</body>
</html>
```

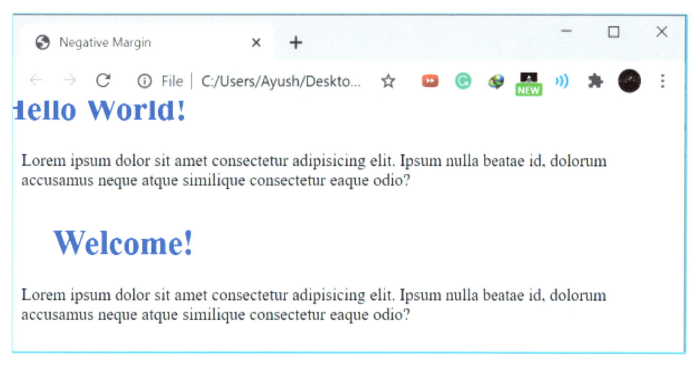

Fig 14.2 Output for Code 14.2

Acknowledgment

Congratulations on reaching the end of this book. I extend my heartfelt gratitude to you for your patience and dedication throughout this journey. I trust you've had an enriching experience, gained valuable insights, and achieved your goals upon completing this book. Thank you for reading.

ABOUT THE AUTHOR

Ayush Raghuwanshi

Ayush Raghuwanshi is a Computer Science Engineer with a passion for writing. As a published author of multiple books, he delves into various genres with creativity and depth. Beyond his literary pursuits, Ayush is an entrepreneur, leveraging his technical background and storytelling skills to create compelling narratives. His experience includes working for a prominent IT conglomerate, where he honed his craft and gained insights that enrich his writing.

Notes

Notes

Notes

Notes

Notes

BOOKS BY THIS AUTHOR

Decoding Html5: Learn To Create Beautiful Websites In 7 Days

The first book in the sequel of '7 Days to Web Mastery' series is 'DECODING HTML5: Learn to Create Beautiful Websites in 7 Days'.

In today's rapidly evolving business landscape, embracing the digital realm is no longer an option but a necessity. As the famous adage goes, "If you don't take your business online, soon you are going out of business." In the 21st century, having a compelling online presence is vital for reaching a broader customer base on a global scale. This is where "DECODING HTML5" comes in.

Whether you're a seasoned entrepreneur or a curious student, this book is your ultimate resource for mastering web development. With its straightforward approach and user-friendly applications, this comprehensive guide empowers you to create your own websites from scratch, regardless of your prior knowledge in the field. No complex jargon or confusing concepts—just a practical, step-by-step process to unleash your creativity and unleash the potential of the online world.

This must-read book delves into the fundamentals of web development, covering everything. Each chapter is thoughtfully designed to break down complex concepts into easily digestible chunks, ensuring an enjoyable learning experience for all readers. As you progress through the book, you'll witness your skills grow and your confidence soar.

While the benefits of web development are universal, this book particularly caters to students with a keen interest in the field. It provides a solid foundation for those eager to embark on a career in web development, offering insights and practical techniques that go beyond what traditional educational resources provide. By mastering the art of website creation, you'll gain a competitive edge over your peers and stand out in the ever-advancing digital landscape.

"DECODING HTML5" is not just a book—it's your gateway to unlocking the vast potential of online success. Start your journey today and equip yourself with the skills needed to thrive in the digital age. Your business, your dreams, and your future await within these pages.

www.ingramcontent.com/pod-product-compliance
Lightning Source LLC
Chambersburg PA
CBHW041434050326
40690CB00003B/543